Sue Goes to the Store

Isabella Ridolfi

ROSEN
COMMON CORE
READERS

Rosen Classroom™

New York

Published in 2013 by The Rosen Publishing Group, Inc.
29 East 21st Street, New York, NY 10010

Book Design: Katelyn Londino

Photo Credits: Cover Indeed/ABSODELS/Getty Images; p. 4 mangostock/Shutterstock.com; pp. 5, 16 (building with shops) Kenneth Sponsler/Shutterstock.com; pp. 6, 15 (grocery store employee) © iStockphoto.com/asiseeit; p. 7 © iStockphoto.com/fotofrog; pp. 8, 15 (florist) Ryan McVay/Lifesize/Getty Images; pp. 9, 15 (flower shop) kanvag/Shutterstock.com; pp. 10, 15 (pet store employee) Yuri Arcurs/Shutterstock.com; pp. 11, 15 (pet store) © iStockphoto.com/aluxum; pp. 12, 15 (book store employee) corepics/Shutterstock.com; pp. 13, 15, 16 (bookstore) Yellow Dog Productions/Digital Vision/Getty Images; p. 14 maska/Shutterstock.com; pp. 15, 16 (grocery store) Kenneth V. Pilon/Shutterstock.com.

ISBN: 978-1-4488-8737-8
6-pack ISBN: 978-1-4488-8738-5

Manufactured in the United States of America

CPSIA Compliance Information: Batch #WS12RC: For further information contact Rosen Publishing, New York, New York at 1-800-237-9932.

Word Count: 107

Contents

Sue knows many people
who work in her neighborhood.

Sue likes to shop.

Her neighborhood has many stores.

Sue knows Mr. Williams.
He works at the grocery store.

Sue goes to the grocery store.
She buys milk.

Sue knows Mr. Thomas.
He works at the garden store.

Sue goes to the garden store.
She sees flowers.

Sue knows Mr. Green.
He works at the pet store.

Sue goes to the pet store.
She gets a goldfish!

Sue knows Miss Morris.
She works at the bookstore.

Sue goes to the bookstore.
She finds many books.

Do you like to shop?
What stores do you like to go to?

Sue's Shopping Trip
grocery store
garden store
pet store
bookstore

Words to Know

bookstore

grocery store

neighborhood

Index